THE EDITOR'S COPY

51 Laws for
Scaling Success
in Business

SINA   AZARI

all **Mindset**

neural connections representing progress and limitless potential.

THE EDITOR'S COPY

51 Laws for
Scaling Success
in Business

Copyright © 2025 *all* Mindset

All Rights Reserved. No part of this book may be reproduced or transmitted in any form or by any means, electronic, or mechanical, including photocopying or recording, or by an information storage and retrieval system, without permission in writing by the author. All translations of this work must be approved in writing by the author. Please contact @*all*mindset for permission to translate and distribution agreements.

Printed in the United States of America.

To order copies in volume, book speaking events or request customized corporate trainings applying The 51 Laws from "The Editor's Copy" for your organization, please email media@allmindset.com.

First Edition

All Mindset
8285 E Santa Ana Cyn Rd.
Suite 135 MB213
Anaheim, CA. 92808

TABLE OF CONTENTS

Preface .... page 10
Introduction .... page 12

Part 1: The Leadership Mindset (Laws 1-10)
.... pages 14-24

1. The Psychology of Success: Thinking Like a Leader

2. Missionaries vs. Mercenaries: Leading with Purpose

3. The Tenacity Factor: Why Persistence is a Superpower

4. Confidence is the Memory of Success

5. Leading from the Front: Setting the Tone for Growth

6. Embracing Volatility: How Uncertainty Fuel Innovation

7. Chess Player, Not Chess Piece: Taking Control of Your Business

8. The High-Standards Principle: The Universe Meets You Where You Are

9. The Second Half Starts at 40: Reinventing Leadership

10. The Power of Vision: Creating a Future That Pulls You Forward

Part 2: Scaling Leadership and Influence (Laws 11-20)
.... pages 25-35

11. Delegation as a Growth Strategy: The Art of Letting Go

12. Leading Through Leverage: How to Make Your Business Work for You

13. Time is Power: Mastering the Schedule for Maximum Efficiency

14. Titles are for Books—Leadership is About Impact

15. The Leadership Paradox: When Strength Becomes a Weakness

16. Staying Consistent: How Small Habits Create Exponential Growth

17. Action Crushes Anxiety: Why Movement Creates Clarity

18. The Speed Principle: Why High-Performing Leaders Move Fast

19. Overcoming Resistance: Handling Setbacks and Failures

20. The Leadership Ecosystem: Surrounding Yourself with Excellence

Part 3: Business Growth & Execution (Laws 21-35)

.... pages 36-55

21. Scaling Through Systems: Building a Business That Runs Itself

22. The Appointment Economy: Why Your Calendar Dictates Your Revenue

23. Value vs. Cost: The Psychology of Selling Premium Products

24. Incremental vs. Exponential: Choosing a Growth Trajectory

25. The Variability Principle: Why Success is Not Linear

26. Know Your Rate Per Hour: Time as Your Most Valuable Asset

27. Write the Narrative vs. Listening to It: Controlling Your Business Story

28. Efficiency is Your Compass, Results Are Your Currency

29. Selling with Integrity: The Key to Long-Term Business Success

30. Capital is Abundant: Positioning Yourself for Investment

31. The Master's Discipline: How Enthusiasm Fuels Mastery

32. Productivity vs. Creativity: Wake Up Early, Stay Up Late

33. The Difference Between Influence and Authority in Leadership

34. Strategic Thinking: How Leaders Make High-Impact Decisions

35. The Importance of Personal Branding in Leadership

Part 4: The Leadership Legacy (Laws 36-51)
.... pages 56-74

36. The Leadership Ripple Effect: How Your Actions Impact Generations

37. Never Wait for a Seat at the Table—Build Your Own

38. The Illusion of Progress: You Could Be Losing So Slowly That You Think You're Winning

39. Mastering Emotional Intelligence: Leadership is About People, Not Just Profits

40. The Compounding Effect of Raising Your Leadership Game

41. Staying Active, Attractive, and Effective as a Leader

42. The Power of Reflection: Why Great Leaders Take Time to Think

43. The Ultimate Leadership Lesson: Remember Why You Started

44. The Full Potential Principle: The Other Side of Fear is Where Success Lives

45. Passion and Persistence: The Two Forces Behind Long-Term Leadership

46. Thinking Beyond Short-Term Wins: Travel at a Higher Frequency

47. Leadership and Age: Experience, Adaptability, and Lifelong Learning

48. The Key to Leadership Longevity: Avoiding Burnout and Staying Inspired

49. From Business Builder to Industry Leader: Expanding Your Influence

50. The Difference Between Leading and Managing: The Final Leadership Lesson

51. Leadership is Not About Taking Power—It's About Taking Over

Final Thoughts / Applying The Laws ...... pages 75+

PREFACE

Success in business is not an accident—it is a process, a formula, and often a set of unwritten rules followed by those who scale to the top. Over the years, I've had the privilege of working with industry leaders, high-performing sales teams, and visionary entrepreneurs, each with their own unique approach to growth. Yet, through all these experiences, I found that the most successful individuals weren't just talented or lucky. They understood and applied certain principles—laws, if you will—that enabled them to scale their businesses strategically and sustainably.

This book, The Editor's Copy: 51 Laws to Scaling Success in Business, is the culmination of those insights. It is a roadmap designed for entrepreneurs, executives, and professionals looking to elevate their business to new heights. These 51 laws are not theories or abstract ideas; they are tested, battle-proven strategies that have driven real-world results across industries.

Why The Editor's Copy? Because in business, much like in writing, the first draft is never the final masterpiece. Success requires refining, editing, and sharpening your strategies over time. Every great leader, like every great author, understands the power of revision—cutting what doesn't work, doubling down on what does, and continuously improving.

Each chapter distills a key law of scaling—whether it's leveraging strategic partnerships, mastering sales psychology, or building a resilient brand. Some of these laws will confirm what you already know, while others may challenge your assumptions. But all of them are designed to help you avoid costly mistakes, accelerate growth, and position yourself as a leader in your industry.

My goal with this book is simple: to give you the ultimate "editor's copy" of success, refined by experience, sharpened by results, and ready for you to implement immediately. Whether you're just starting out or looking to break through a plateau, these laws will serve as your blueprint for sustainable and scalable success.

You don't have to read this book from start to finish—think of it as a leadership toolkit. Whenever you face a challenge in your business or leadership journey, open this book, find the relevant law, and apply it immediately.

Let's get started.

— Sina Azari

Introduction: The Laws for Leadership & Growth

Leadership isn't about titles, authority, or power—it's about **influence, action, and results.** In today's fast-moving business world, leaders who **understand how to scale themselves and their businesses** will thrive, while those who refuse to adapt will be left behind. The Editor's Copy: 51 Laws for Scaling Success in Business is not just another business book. It's a **strategic blueprint for leaders who want to grow their influence, build high-performance teams, and scale their businesses exponentially.**

This is designed for:

- **Entrepreneurs & business owners** who want to scale sustainably

- **Corporate leaders & executives** who need to inspire and lead effectively

- **Sales professionals & consultants** who want to master influence

- **Anyone in leadership** looking to elevate their mindset and execution

Each chapter provides **a fundamental law of leadership,** backed by **real-world applications, proven psychological principles, and high-performance strategies.** You don't have to read this book from start to finish—think of it as a **leadership toolkit.** Whenever you face a challenge in your business or leadership journey, open this book, find the relevant law, and apply it immediately. Now, let's dive into the **first law of leadership—developing the psychology of success.**

PART 1: THE LEADERSHIP MINDSET

(Laws 1-10)

LAW 1

he Psychology of Success:
Thinking Like a Leader

Great leaders think differently. They don't react—they **respond with strategy**. They don't chase every opportunity—they **create leverage.**

Success starts with **mindset mastery.** Here's what separates elite leaders from the rest:

- **They are proactive, not reactive.** They anticipate problems before they arise.
- **They operate with urgency.** Speed of execution is a competitive advantage.
- **They lead with confidence.** Confidence is the memory of past successes.
- **They take ownership.** No excuses, no blaming—only solutions.

How to Apply This Law:

1. **Start thinking exponentially.** Don't focus on incremental growth—ask, "How can I scale 10x?"

2. **Control your environment.** Surround yourself with people who push you to grow.

3. **Build momentum.** Take action daily—**action crushes anxiety.**

4. **Master your time.** Your business is a reflection of how you manage your time.

LAW 2

issionaries vs. Mercenaries: Leading with Purpose

There are two types of business leaders: **missionaries and mercenaries.**

•   **Mercenaries** chase profits, operate transactionally, and focus on short-term wins.

•   **Missionaries** lead with vision, build movements, and create lasting impact.

If you want **true business success, you must become a missionary leader. Your mission attracts people, builds culture, and fuels long-term growth.**

How to Apply This Law:

•   **Define your mission.** Why does your business exist beyond making money?

•   **Communicate your vision.** People follow clarity, not confusion.

•   **Make purpose your advantage.** When tough times hit, your mission keeps you moving.

LAW 3

he Tenacity Factor:
Why Persistence is a Superpower

Success is rarely about raw talent—it's about **tenacity**. The ability to **keep moving forward** when obstacles arise separates those who scale from those who stall.

Every successful business leader has faced **rejection, failure, and setbacks**. The difference? **They kept going.**

How to Apply This Law:

- **Adopt a "No Plan B" mentality.** Burn the boats—commit fully.
- **Reframe failure as feedback.** Every setback is a setup for a comeback.
- **Maintain relentless consistency.** Success is a daily habit, not a one-time event.

LAW 4

onfidence is the Memory of Success

Confidence is not something you're born with—it's something you build through **consistent action and repeated success.** The best leaders understand that confidence is simply **trust in their own ability to figure things out.**

The Formula for Confidence:
- **Competence → Repetition → Success → Confidence**
- Every time you take action and succeed, **your brain records it.**
- The **more you succeed, the stronger your belief** in yourself becomes.
- The trick? **Create small, daily wins to reinforce your confidence loop.**

How to Apply This Law:
1. **Stack small wins.** Break big goals into bite-sized victories.
2. **Review past successes.** Keep a "success journal" to reinforce confidence.
3. **Take action quickly.** The faster you move, the less room fear has to grow.
4. **Eliminate negative self-talk.** Leaders don't entertain self-doubt.

LAW 5

eading from the Front: Setting the Tone for Growth

As a leader, you set the **pace, culture, and energy** of your business. If you're disciplined, **your team will be disciplined.** If you procrastinate, **your business will stagnate.**

Leadership is About Modeling Behavior:

• Your **work ethic** sets the standard for your team.

• Your **communication** determines how well your vision is followed.

• Your **decision-making speed** influences how fast your business grows.

How to Apply This Law:

• **Set the tone.** Your business is a reflection of your habits.

• **Lead by example.** Never expect others to do what you won't.

• **Move with urgency**. Success loves speed.

LAW 6

Embracing Volatility: How Uncertainty Fuels Innovation

Many leaders fear **uncertainty**, but the best embrace it. The truth is, **business is inherently volatile**—markets shift, competitors evolve, and customers change. Great leaders don't just **survive change**—they **use it as fuel for innovation.**

How to Apply This Law:
- **Anticipate change**. Always look 3-5 years ahead.
- **Stay adaptable**. Pivot quickly when opportunities arise.
- **Turn chaos into opportunity**. Market shifts create room for new leaders.

LAW 7

Chess Player, Not Chess Piece: Taking Control of Your Business

There are two types of leaders:
- **Chess pieces** react to the board and get moved around.
- **Chess players** think ahead and control the game.

To scale a business, you need to move from being **a worker inside your business to a strategist leading it**.

How to Apply This Law:

- **Think long-term.** Make moves today that benefit you 5 years from now.
- **Play offense, not defense.** Proactive leaders shape markets.
- **Work on your business, not just in it.** Focus on strategy over execution.

LAW 8

he High-Standards Principle: The Universe Meets You Where You Are

You don't get what you want—you get what you **tolerate.** High-performing leaders **set high standards** for themselves, their teams, and their businesses.

How to Apply This Law:

• **Audit your environment**. Who and what are you tolerating?

• **Raise your expectations**. Demand excellence in execution.

• **Hold people accountable.** Success is built on standards, not suggestions.

LAW 9

he Second Half Starts at 40: Reinventing Leadership

Most people believe success has an expiration date—it doesn't. Many of the most successful leaders **built their greatest achievements after 40.**

How to Apply This Law:

• **See age as an advantage**. Experience compounds over time.

• **Stay adaptable.** Reinvention is key to long-term success.

• **Never stop learning.** Growth doesn't end—it evolves.

LAW 10

The Power of Vision: Creating a Future That Pulls You Forward

A strong **vision** makes leadership easier. When people know **where you're going and why it matters**, they follow naturally.

How to Apply This Law:

- **Clarify your vision.** Write down where you want to be in 5, 10, and 20 years.

- **Communicate it constantly**. Repetition reinforces belief.

- **Align actions with vision.** Every decision should serve the bigger picture.

PART 2: SCALING LEADERSHIP AND INFLUENCE

(Laws 11-20)

LAW 11

Delegation as a Growth Strategy: The Art of Letting Go

The biggest bottleneck in business growth is **a leader who refuses to delegate.**

The 3-Step Delegation Process:

1. **Eliminate**. What tasks shouldn't be done at all?
2. **Automate**. What tasks can be done by software?
3. **Delegate**. What tasks can be done by others?

How to Apply This Law:

- **Stop micromanaging.** Trust your team.

- **Hire people smarter than you**. Your job is to lead, not to do everything.

- **Focus on high-leverage tasks.** Only do what moves the business forward.

LAW 12

eading Through Leverage: How to Make Your Business Work for You

Most people work harder for their business—but smart leaders get their business to work harder for them.

How to Apply This Law:

- **Leverage systems**. Automate, delegate, and optimize.
- **Leverage people**. Build a team that operates independently.
- **Leverage time**. Focus on tasks that create exponential results.

LAW 13

**ime is Power: Mastering the Schedule for Maximum Efficiency**

Time is Power: Mastering the Schedule for Maximum Efficiency Time is your most valuable resource—how you use it **determines your success.**

How to Apply This Law:

- **Protect your calendar.** Prioritize high-impact activities.
- **Say no often.** Every "yes" is a "no" to something else.
- **Use time blocks.** Dedicate hours for deep work.

LAW 14

itles are for Books—Leadership is About Impact

A title doesn't make you a leader—your **actions, influence, and results** do.

How to Apply This Law:
- **Lead by example.** People follow action, not words.
- **Prioritize impact over status.** Focus on results, not position.
- **Build a reputation for leadership.** Influence speaks louder than titles.

LAW 15

The Leadership Paradox: When Strength Becomes a Weakness

A strength, when overused, can become a liability.

- **Confidence → Arrogance**
- **Decisiveness → Impulsiveness**
- **Persistence → Stubbornness**

How to Apply This Law:

- **Stay self-aware.** Recognize when strengths become excesses.
- **Seek feedback.** Smart leaders listen to outside perspectives.
- Balance your traits. **Success is about adaptability.**

LAW 16

taying Consistent: How SmallHabits Create Exponential Growth

Success isn't built on big moments—it's built on **daily habits, repeated over time.** The best leaders aren't the most talented; they're the most **consistent.**

The Power of Consistency:

• Small actions, repeated daily, **compound into massive success.**

• Inconsistency creates **doubt, distrust, and instability.**

• The leaders who grow the fastest **commit to disciplined execution.**

How to Apply This Law:

1. **Commit to daily execution.** Do what matters every single day.
2. **Track progress.** Measure success with key metrics.
3. **Build accountability.** Surround yourself with people who push you forward.

LAW 17

ction Crushes Anxiety: Why Movement Creates Clarity

Overthinking is the enemy of success. Leaders who act **gain momentum** while those who hesitate **stay stuck.**

Why Action Matters More Than Perfection:

- **Clarity comes from movement.** You don't need all the answers to start.
- **Action destroys fear**. The more you do, the less you doubt.
- **Momentum creates breakthroughs**. Small wins lead to big results.

How to Apply This Law:

- **Decide fast.** 80% decisions today are better than 100% perfect decisions later.
- **Take imperfect action.** Progress > Perfection.
- **Trust that clarity will come.** Start, then refine as you go.

LAW 18

he Speed Principle: Why High-Performing Leaders Move Fast

Slow leaders get **outpaced, outperformed, and outgrown**. The best leaders **move fast, learn fast, and adjust fast.**

How to Apply This Law:

1. **Make fast decisions**. Waiting is often more costly than making a wrong move.
2. **Cut unnecessary steps**. Eliminate delays and inefficiencies.
3. **Focus on execution, not over-planning**. The best plan is worthless without action.

LAW 19

Overcoming Resistance: Handling Setbacks and Failures

Every leader faces resistance—**the difference is how they respond to it.**

How to Apply This Law:

- **Reframe failure.** See it as feedback, not defeat.

- **Stay resilient.** The ability to push through obstacles is what defines leadership.

- **Turn resistance into fuel.** Doubters and setbacks should drive you harder.

LAW 20

he Leadership Ecosystem: Surrounding Yourself with Excellence

Your **network determines your net worth**. The best leaders **build environments that accelerate their growth**.

How to Apply This Law:
1. **Audit your circle.** Are the people around you lifting you up or holding you back?
2. **Join high-level networks.** Get into rooms where growth happens.
3. **Invest in relationships.** Leadership is about **who you know and who knows you**.

PART 3: BUSINESS GROWTH & EXECUTION
(LAWS 21-35)

LAW 21

caling Through Systems: Building a Business That Runs Itself

If your business **relies on you, you don't own a business—you own a job.** Leaders **scale through systems, not effort.**

How to Apply This Law:
- **Document everything.** Turn repeatable tasks into processes.
- **Automate what you can.** Reduce manual work with smart tools.
- **Build a self-sustaining team.** Your business should thrive without you.

LAW 22

he Appointment Economy: Why Your Calendar Dictates Your Revenue

Business growth is an appointment game. As in, get up, get in and get out. Having set appointments is **the most critical step to sustaining and growing your business**. Strategically manage your time and appointments to directly impact your income and success.

How to Apply This Law:

1. Prioritize High-Value Meetings. Block time for revenue-generating activities like sales calls and client consultations.

2. Use a structured calendar. Allocate specific slots for lead generation or follow ups.

3. Automate & Systematize Your Booking Process. Use scheduling tools and applications. Ensure follow up reminders to **reduce no shows.**

4. Qualify Appointments Before Booking. Use a pre-qualification process such as a form, email or quick call. **Pre-screen protecting your time.**

5. Maximize Client Appointments for Upselling & Referrals. Prepare before every meeting to identify cross-sell and upsell opportunities.

6. Limit Free Consultations & Unpaid Meetings. Consider charging for strategy sessions or consultations to filter serious prospects.

7. Track Appointment Metrics & Optimize. Monitor your "appointment to revenue ratio". Calculate how many meetings lead to a closed deal. **Adjust your schedule as needed.**

LAW 23

 alue vs. Cost: The Psychology of Selling Premium Products

People don't buy based on price—they buy based on **perceived value.**

How to Apply This Law:
•	**Focus on outcomes, not features.** Sell transformation, not transactions.
•	**Price high and deliver high.** Cheap attracts cheap—great attracts great.
•	**Build authority.** The stronger your brand, the less price matters. "

LAW 24

Incremental vs. Exponential: Choosing a Growth Trajectory

Most businesses grow **incrementally**—but the real winners grow **exponentially.**

How to Apply This Law:

- **Think 10x, not 10%.** Ask: "How can I scale this in a massive way?"
- **Leverage people, technology, and capital.** Scale requires smart resource use.
- **Play the long game.** Exponential growth compounds over time.

LAW 25

The Variability Principle: Why Success is Not Linear

Success is **not a straight path**—it's a **rollercoaster**.

How to Apply This Law:
1. **Expect fluctuations**. Don't panic when results dip.
2. **Stay adaptable**. Pivot quickly when needed.
3. **Play the macro game**. Focus on **long-term trends**, not short-term noise.

LAW 26

now Your Rate Per Hour:
Time as Your Most Valuable Asset

Time is more valuable than money—**you can't make more of it.**

How to Apply This Law:

- **Calculate your hourly rate.** Work only on tasks worth your time.
- **Outsource low-value tasks.** Pay others so you can focus on growth.
- **Use leverage.** Invest time where it has the highest return.

LAW 27

rite the Narrative vs. Listening to It: Controlling Your Business Story

If you don't control your story, **the market will define it for you.**

How to Apply This Law:

1. **Own your brand message.** Be intentional about what you represent.

2. **Control the perception.** Consistently communicate your vision.

3. **Be the storyteller, not the character.** Shape your market's view of you.

LAW 28

Efficiency is Your Compass, Results Are Your Currency

Success is about **working smarter, not just harder.**

How to Apply This Law:

- **Optimize workflows.** Remove unnecessary complexity.
- **Measure output, not just effort.** Results matter more than hours worked.
- **Run your business like an elite athlete trains—every week should count.**

LAW 29

Selling with Integrity: The Key to Long-Term Business Success

The best leaders **build trust, not just transactions.**

How to Apply This Law:
- **Focus on service.** Solve problems, don't just sell.
- **Be transparent.** Honesty builds lifelong customers.
- **Play the long game.** Ethical business wins in the long run.

LAW 30

Capital is Abundant: Positioning Yourself for Investment

There's more money in the world than opportunities—**become an opportunity.**

How to Apply This Law:
- **Think like an investor.** Position your business for funding.
- **Build assets, not just revenue.** Long-term value attracts capital.
- **Create undeniable value.** If your business is great, money will find you.

LAW 31

he Master's Discipline –
How Enthusiasm Fuels Mastery

The path to mastery isn't just about repetition—it's **about maintaining enthusiasm** for the fundamentals. The best leaders don't get bored with the basics; they **find new ways** to **refine and elevate** their craft.

Why This Matters:

•   Most **people lose interest** in skills or habits before they **achieve mastery.**

•   The **best performers fall in love with the process**, not just the outcome.

•   **Mastery comes from deliberate practice**, not passive repetition.

How to Apply This Law:

1.   **Recommit to the basics.** Identify one fundamental skill you've neglected and **focus on improving** it.

2.   **Make repetition exciting**. Approach routine tasks with the mindset of a scientist—how can you refine them further?

3.   **Keep learning.** Even at the highest levels, **continuous improvement separates the great from the good.**

LAW 32

Productivity vs. Creativity – Wake Up Early, Stay Up Late

Productivity and **creativity operate on different cycles.** The best leaders **learn to balance structured execution** (mornings) with creative thinking (late nights).

Why This Matters:

- **Mornings are best for execution**, planning, and disciplined action.
- **Evenings are best for creative thinking**, brainstorming, and problem-solving.
- Understanding this balance lets you **maximize both efficiency and innovation.**

How to Apply This Law:

1. **Protect your mornings** for execution. Do your most critical tasks early when your mind is fresh.
2. Use nights for creativity. Brainstorm ideas, write, strategize, and **reflect when distractions are minimal.**
3. **Understand your rhythms**. Adjust your schedule to when you're naturally most **productive vs creative.**

LAW 33

he Difference Between Influence and Authority in Leadership

Authority comes from your position, but **influence comes from your ability to inspire action.** The best leaders **maximize influence**, not just authority.

Why This Matters:

• **Authority is given**—it comes from titles, promotions, or company hierarchy.

• **Influence is earned**—it comes from trust, credibility, and leadership presence.

• **True leaders don't rely on authority**—they inspire action through influence.

How to Apply This Law:

1. **Lead with trust and credibility.** People follow who they respect, not just who they report to.

2. **Master persuasion.** Influence is about communication, clarity, and conviction.

3. **Serve others.** The more you help people, the more they willingly follow your leadership.

LAW 34

trategic Thinking – How Leaders Make High-Impact Decisions

Most people react—**great leaders strategize**. Strategic thinking is the ability to **step back, see the bigger picture,** and **make calculated moves** that shape the future.

Why This Matters:

- **Leaders who only react stay stuck** in the short-term.
- **Strategic thinkers play the long game** and anticipate trends.
- Every major business **breakthrough comes from proactive decision-making**, not reactive firefighting.

How to Apply This Law:

1. **Schedule time for strategic thinking.** Block at least one hour per week to **analyze long-term goals.**
2. **Ask better questions**. Shift from "What should I do today?" to "What will matter in five years?"
3. **Look for leverage points**. The best decisions produce exponential impact, not just incremental progress.

LAW 35

The Importance of Personal Branding in Leadership

Your **personal brand is your leadership identity.** It determines how people perceive you, the opportunities you attract, and the influence you wield—both inside and outside your organization. In today's world, **leaders must intentionally shape their personal brand** to establish authority, credibility, and long-term impact.

Why This Matters:
- **People follow leaders they recognize and trust.**
- **A strong personal brand creates more influence than a title.**
- **Your online and offline reputation precedes you.** The world forms opinions about you before you even walk into the room.

A personal brand is **not about self-promotion**—it's about being **visible, valuable, and memorable** in your industry and leadership space.

How to Build a Powerful Personal Brand as a Leader

1. Define Your Leadership Identity.

- If you don't define who you are as a leader, **the world will do it for you.** Your personal brand should reflect:

- **Your core leadership values** (Integrity, innovation, service, execution, etc.)

- **Your expertise and industry authority** (What do you want to be known for?)

- **Your leadership philosophy** (How do you lead and inspire people?

2. Establish Thought Leadership

Your expertise is only valuable if others know about it. The most influential leaders actively **share knowledge** to position themselves as industry authorities.

Ways to Build Thought Leadership:

- **Write articles or LinkedIn posts** on leadership, business strategy, or your industry.

- **Start a podcast, blog, or video series** to share your leadership lessons.

- **Speak on panels, webinars, or interviews** to showcase expertise.

- **Publish case studies, white papers, or books** that demonstrate thought leadership.

3. Build an Authentic Digital Presence

A leader's **personal brand exists online—whether they control it or not.** Your social media, interviews, and online mentions shape how the world perceives you.

- **LinkedIn** – Thought leadership posts, articles, and networking.

- **Twitter/X** – Industry insights, leadership lessons, and engagement with thought leaders.

- **Instagram/Youtube** – Behind-the-scenes leadership moments, interviews, or personal branding content.

- **Personal Website** – A space to showcase your **expertise, media features, and leadership philosophy.**

4. Network & Build Strategic Relationships

Your **personal brand is amplified by who you associate with.** Surround yourself with **high-level leaders, mentors, and peers who challenge you to grow.**

- Attend leadership events, summits, and networking opportunities.

- Build **authentic** relationships (not just transactional networking).

- Partner with other industry leaders on **collaborations, interviews, or joint projects.**

5. Be Authentic – Your Story is Your Brand

People don't connect with **perfection—they connect with authenticity.** The best leaders share their **failures, lessons, and real-life experiences**—not just their achievements.

- **Show vulnerability.** Leaders who admit struggles gain more trust.

- **Share behind-the-scenes moments.** Give insight into your leadership journey.

- **Stay true to your values.** People can sense when a brand is fake.

The best leaders aren't just known for what they do—they are known for how they lead. If you don't intentionally build your personal brand, **you are leaving opportunities on the table.**

PART 4: THE LEADERSHIP LEGACY
(Laws 36-51)

Leadership isn't just about growing a business—it's about creating lasting impact that outlives you. The best leaders don't just succeed for themselves—they empower others, build systems, and leave behind a legacy of excellence.

LAW 36

he Leadership Ripple Effect: How Your Actions Impact Generations

Every action you take as a leader **sets a ripple effect into motion.** The businesses you build, the people you mentor, and the standards you set will **influence others for years to come.**

How to Apply This Law:

- **Think long-term.** What will people remember you for in 10, 20, or 50 years?
- **Be intentional.** Your decisions shape more lives than you realize.
- **Invest in people.** The strongest legacy is **the leaders you develop.**

LAW 37

Never Wait for a Seat at the Table—Build Your Own

The biggest mistake leaders make? **Waiting for permission to lead.** Instead of hoping for an invitation, **create your own opportunities.**

How to Apply This Law:

- **Stop waiting.** If an opportunity doesn't exist, create it.
- **Build authority.** Position yourself as an industry leader.
- **Control your future.** True leadership means making your own rules.

LAW 38

he Illusion of Progress: You Could Be Losing So Slowly That You Think You're Winning

Many businesses **fail gradually**—not suddenly. They mistake **stability for success** and don't realize they're falling behind.

How to Apply This Law:

• **Measure real growth.** Are you improving, or just staying busy?

• **Disrupt yourself**. Before the market disrupts you.

• **Look at the scoreboard.** Focus on **real results, not effort.**

LAW 39

astering Emotional Intelligence: Leadership is About People, Not Just Profits

Business isn't just about numbers—it's about **people**. Leaders who lack emotional intelligence **fail to inspire, connect, and build trust**.

How to Apply This Law:
• **Listen more than you speak**. Great leaders understand before reacting.
• **Manage emotions.** Respond strategically, not emotionally.
• **Lead with empathy.** People follow those who **genuinely care**.

LAW 40

The Compounding Effect of Raising Your Leadership Game

Leadership is **not static**—it's a **lifelong process of improvement.** Every small upgrade in your leadership ability **compounds into massive success over time**.

How to Apply This Law:

- **Level up constantly.** Never stop learning, evolving, and growing.
- **Surround yourself with better leaders.** Growth happens in the right environments.
- **Teach others.** The best way to master something is to mentor others.

LAW 41

Staying Active, Attractive, and Effective as a Leader

Great leaders **prioritize their energy, health, and presence**. If you're burnt out, uninspired, or physically drained, your leadership suffers.

How to Apply This Law:

• **Stay physically active.** Energy is a leader's secret weapon.

• **Continue to learn.** Stay mentally sharp and adaptable.

• **Take care of yourself.** A leader's greatest asset is their mind and body.

LAW 42

he Power of Reflection: Why Great Leaders Take Time to Think

The most successful leaders don't just **work hard**—they **think strategically**. If you're always busy, you're not **making time for big-picture thinking**.

How to Apply This Law:

- **Schedule reflection time.** Step back and analyze your leadership.
- **Ask better questions**. "What's the next big move?"
- **Think before you act.** Wise leaders don't just react—they strategize.

LAW 43

he Ultimate Leadership Lesson: Remember Why You Started

Over time, **leaders can lose sight of their original mission.** The key to long-term success? **Always"reconnect with your WHY**.

How to Apply This Law:
• **Revisit your purpose.** Why did you start this journey?
• **Keep perspective.** Leadership is a privilege, not just a position.
• **Lead with passion.** Passion fuels momentum, even during hard times.

LAW 44

**he Full Potential Principle: The Other Side of Fear is Where Success Lives**

Most people **never reach their full potential** because they stop when they feel fear. True leaders **push past fear and into their greatest breakthroughs.**

How to Apply This Law:

- **Lean into discomfort.** Growth happens in uncertainty.
- **Act despite fear.** Courage is action, not the absence of fear.
- **Expand your limits.** Every time you break through, you level up.

LAW 45

Passion and Persistence: The Two Forces Behind Long-Term Leadership

Talent **fades without effort**. Intelligence **means nothing without execution.** The most successful leaders combine **passion (fuel) with persistence (grit).**

How to Apply This Law:
- **Don't chase quick wins.** Focus on sustainable success.
- **Keep showing up.** Most people quit too soon.
- **Love the process.** The journey is what creates mastery.

LAW 46

hinking Beyond Short-Term Wins: Travel at a Higher Frequency

Short-term thinking leads to **short-term results**. The best leaders **operate on a different level—they see the game 5, 10, or 20 years ahead.**

How to Apply This Law:

- **Zoom out.** What are your 10-year and 20-year goals?
- **Build a legacy, not just a business.** Aim for impact, not just profits.
- **Stay above the noise.** Focus on what truly matters.

LAW 47

Leadership and Age: Experience, Adaptability, and Lifelong Learning

Leadership isn't about age—**it's about experience, adaptability, and continuous learning.**

How to Apply This Law:
- **Use experience wisely.** Learn from past successes and failures.
- **Stay adaptable.** Evolve as industries change.
- **Never stop learning.** The best leaders are always students.

LAW 48

he Key to Leadership Longevity: Avoiding Burnout and Staying Inspired

Great leaders don't just build success—they **sustain it.** Burnout is real, and avoiding it **is key to long-term leadership.**

How to Apply This Law:

- **Pace yourself.** Leadership is a marathon, not a sprint.
- **Find inspiration.** Stay connected to your passion.
- **Take strategic breaks.** Rest and recovery fuel long-term impact.

LAW 49

rom Business Builder to Industry Leader: Expanding Your Influence

The highest level of leadership isn't just **running a business**—it's **shaping an industry**.

How to Apply This Law:

• **Build a personal brand.** Be known as an authority.
• **Expand your reach.** Teach, speak, and share your expertise.
• **Mentor future leaders.** Influence scales when you develop others.

LAW 50

The Difference Between Leading and Managing: The Final Leadership Lesson

Managers maintain—**leaders elevate. Leadership is about vision, influence, and direction.**

How to Apply This Law:

- **Delegate management.** Your job is to lead, not control every detail.
- **Set vision, not just targets.** People follow big missions, not micromanagement.
- **Lead boldly.** The future belongs to those who take action.

LAW 51

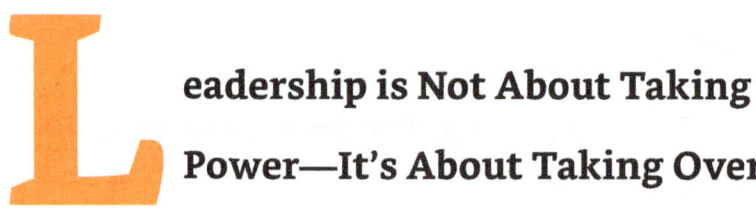

Leadership is Not About Taking Power—It's About Taking Over

True leadership isn't about **securing a title or accumulating power**—it's about **creating undeniable impact and transforming the environment around you.**

Great leaders don't just **enter an industry or business**—they **take full command of the space, redefine the rules, and establish dominance.**

Taking power = Seeking control
Taking over = Owning the space with impact, innovation, and influence

Why This Matters:
• Many leaders focus on **authority and status** rather than **real influence.**
• The best leaders **don't wait to be given power**—they create **a movement that makes them impossible to ignore.**
• Power fades when positions change—**but when you take over an industry, a market, or a mindset, your leadership lasts.**

How to Take Over as a Leader...

(Not Just Seek Power)

1. Focus on Ownership, Not Just Position
- Titles mean nothing if you don't **create massive impact.**
- Own your **business, your expertise, and your leadership influence.**
- **Ask yourself:** Am I aiming for **a job title or an undeniable presence in my field?**

2. Build a Movement, Not Just a Following
- Great leaders **don't just attract followers—they create a vision so strong that people want to be part of it.**
- Apple, Tesla, and Nike aren't just companies—they are **movements people believe in.**
- **To take over, your leadership must stand for something greater than just business success.**

3. Dominate with Innovation & Execution
- You don't take over an industry by copying—you **become the standard by innovating.**
- The best leaders **execute relentlessly, move fast, and don't wait for validation.**
- **Amazon, Netflix, and Airbnb** didn't wait for approval—they **changed the rules of the game.**

4. Expand Your Leadership Beyond One Space
- Power is temporary, but **influence expands across industries, networks, and generations.**
- Many great **leaders didn't limit themselves to one field.**

- Taking over means **building influence that moves across industries, platforms, and markets.**

5. Move with Certainty & Take Bold Risks
- Leaders who **hesitate** get overlooked.
- Those who **own their space with confidence command the market.**
- Taking over requires **decisive action, high standards, and fearlessness.**

This law isn't just about leading—**it's about becoming the leader everyone else follows.** Are you ready to take over?

FINAL THOUGHTS

The Editor's Copy in Action…Leadership is not a position—it is a responsibility. It is the ability to see beyond the present, think strategically, and influence the world around you in a way that is undeniable. **This book has outlined 51 powerful laws designed to help you master your mindset, scale your influence, execute with precision, and leave a lasting legacy.** But here's the truth: Reading about leadership is not enough.

You must act on it. The best leaders do not wait. They move boldly, execute relentlessly, and adapt fearlessly.

The Four Pillars of Leadership Mastery… (Summarizing the Laws)

1. The Leadership Mindset: Shaping the Way You Think & Operate

Key Laws:
- The Psychology of Success – Leaders think in terms of solutions, not problems.
- Missionaries vs. Mercenaries – Purpose-driven leaders create lasting impact.
- Confidence is the Memory of Success – The best leaders build confidence through repeated victories.
- The Master's Discipline – Leaders who sustain enthusiasm for mastery outlast everyone else.
- Taking Over vs. Taking Power – Leadership is not about titles—it's about undeniable impact.

> **Your mindset is the foundation of everything. If you don't think like a leader, nothing else will matter.**

2. Scaling Leadership & Influence: Building a Movement Beyond Yourself

Key Laws:

- Delegation as a Growth Strategy – Your job is not to do everything—it's to lead the people who do.
- The Power of Personal Branding – The strongest leaders have reputations that speak for them.
- The Difference Between Influence and Authority – People follow true influence, not just positions of power.
- Build a Movement, Not Just a Following – Great leaders don't just attract people—they inspire action.
- Networking & Strategic Relationships – Your circle defines your ceiling. Surround yourself with high-level thinkers.

> **Leadership at the highest level is not about you—it's about the impact you create, the influence you build, and the movement you lead.**

3. Business Growth & Execution: Converting Leadership into Results

Key Laws:

- Time is Power – Control your schedule, or someone else will.
- Scaling Through Systems – You do

- Scaling Through Systems – You don't own a business if it collapses without you.
- Productivity vs. Creativity – Structure your days for both execution and vision.
- The Speed Principle – Momentum matters more than perfection. Move fast.
- The Illusion of Progress – Many businesses are slowly failing while they believe they are winning.

Execution is what separates leaders from dreamers. The best ideas mean nothing without relentless implementation.

4. **The Leadership Legacy: Creating Impact That Outlasts You**

Key Laws:
- The Ripple Effect of Leadership – Every action you take sets the tone for future generations.
- The Compounding Effect of Raising Your Leadership Game – 1% daily improvement leads to exponential impact.
- Mastering Emotional Intelligence – Business is about people. Leaders who don't understand people will fail.
- Strategic Thinking & High-Impact Decisions – The best leaders think years ahead, not just months.
- Never Wait for a Seat at the Table—Build Your Own – The strongest leaders create "their own platforms instead of waiting to be recognized.

The ultimate test of leadership is not how much power you gain—it's how much impact you leave behind.

LEADERSHIP CHALLENGE

If you only read these laws and do nothing, nothing will change. Your challenge is simple:

- Pick five laws that resonated the most with you.
- Write down a specific action step for each.
- Execute within the next 30 days.

Execution Over Excuses. This book is not just a guide—it is a blueprint for action.

LEADERSHIP COMMITMENT:

If you are serious about elevating your leadership game, growing your business, and taking over your industry, then commit to the following:

- I will think and act like a leader—every single day.
- I will prioritize execution over excuses.
- I will build something bigger than myself.
- I will lead with impact, integrity, and vision.
- I will not just take power—I will take over.

The world rewards those who execute. Will you take action or just consume information?

The world is full of followers waiting for direction, companies waiting for leaders, and industries waiting for disruptors. Will you be the one to step up? **This is Your Editor's Copy....Are you building on excuses or results?**

About the Author

Sina Azari is a dynamic entrepreneur, sales leader, and industry innovator with over two decades of experience in professional services, technology, and enterprise solutions. Recognized for his expertise in high-performance sales, strategic alliances, and market expansion, Sina has built a reputation for driving growth and transformation in competitive industries.

As a mentor, speaker, and content creator, Sina is passionate about empowering professionals with actionable insights that bridge the gap between ambition and achievement. He has helped countless individuals and businesses navigate the evolving landscape of sales, insurance, and real estate, leveraging cutting-edge strategies to maximize success.

Beyond his professional endeavors, Sina is a dedicated educator, hosting webinars, podcasts, and social media initiatives aimed at fostering industry collaboration and elevating brands. Whether coaching sales teams, consulting for Fortune 500 companies, or building next-generation leaders, his mission remains clear: to inspire, educate, and create lasting impact.

This book is a testament to his journey, experiences, and hard-earned wisdom—designed to equip readers with the knowledge, mindset, and strategies to reach new heights in their own careers.

Acknowledgements

Writing *The Editor's Copy* has been an incredible journey, and I couldn't have done it alone.

First and foremost, I want to thank my family and close friends for their unwavering support, patience, and belief in me. Your encouragement kept me going through moments of self-doubt.

To my mentors and colleagues—your insights, advice, and experiences have shaped not only this book but also my career. The lessons I've learned from you are reflected in every page.

A special thank you to my editor, designer, and publishing team—your expertise brought this book to life in ways I could have never imagined.

To the business leaders, entrepreneurs, and sales professionals who continue to push boundaries and redefine success—this book is for you. May it serve as a guide and a reminder that growth is an ongoing process, shaped by the right strategies and mindset.

And finally, to **you**, the reader—thank you for investing your time in these pages. I hope this book empowers you to scale your business, sharpen your approach, and achieve the success you envision.

Here's to the next chapter—yours.

—Sina Azari

**"Success isn't about what you know—
it's about how fast you implement."**

Please connect and tag the author at the following social media channels as you share and repost your favorite laws.

https://www.instagram.com/ceoaccredited

https://www.Linkedin.Com/In/Sinaazari

Or by visiting:

www.SinaAzari.com

Made in the USA
Las Vegas, NV
27 February 2025